First published in 2006 by
Franklin Watts
338 Euston Road
London NW1 3BH

Franklin Watts Australia
Hachette Children's Books
Level 17/207 Kent Street
Sydney NSW 2000

Text copyright © Ruth Thomson 2006
Photographs copyright © Neil Thomson 2006

Series editor: Rachel Cooke
Series designer: Holly Mann
Art Director: Rachel Hamdi
Consultants: Jo Hollins, Education Officer
at Rockware Glass and Ben Stone,
Recycling Officer at British Glass

Additional Photographs
Thanks are due to the following for kind
permission to reproduce photographs:
Madeleine Boulesteix: 19 (top); Dichrolicious
(Richard and Diana Sewell): 18 (bottom);
Green Bottle Unit: 27; Rockware Glass: 8
(centre), 22- 23; Recycle now: front and back
endpapers, 12 (top), 20 (bottom left), 21 (left)

ISBN 07496 6105 4

A CIP catalogue record for this book is
available from the British Library.

Dewey Decimal Classification Number: 666'.1

Printed in China

Acknowledgements
The author and publisher wish to thank the
following people for their help with this book:
John Ball, Merle Ribeiro, Jonathan Davids and
Timothy William at the *Carpenter's Shop*, Cape
Town, South Africa; Mohamed Hassan at the
Eldaur Glass House, Cairo; Abdel Moula Al
Rachid; Jo Hollins, Zoe Cross and Simon
Morgan of *Rockware Glass*, Knottingley, West
Yorkshire; Martin Goodrich and *Green Bottle
Unit*, London; *Aurora Vidros*, Curitiba, Brazil;
Yole Milani Medeiros, Osama Ali, Sue Adler,
Mark Watson and Mary-Jane Wilkins; also
Oliver Binks, Joe Knight, Rebbekah Channer,
Emma Lewin, Arun Simpson and Beatrice
Chamberlain-Kent for their participation
as models.

re-using

Glass

Ruth Thomson

Photography by Neil Thomson

W
FRANKLIN WATTS
LONDON·SYDNEY

Contents

Words printed in **bold** are explained in the glossary.

What is glass like?

It is easy to see why glass is such a useful **material**.
Almost everywhere you look – at home, at school
or in the street – you can spot things made of glass.

Glass is see-through.
It lets in light, but keeps out
wind and rain.

Glass does not become soggy
or leak when it gets wet.
That's why glass bottles are useful for
storing **liquids**, such as juice and oil.

A lens is made of curved glass. It is thicker in the middle than around the edges. This bends light to make things look bigger than they really are.

Glass is hard and smooth. It is easy to clean, so it is safe and **hygienic** for drinks and food.

Glass does not mix with or change anything it touches. Food in sealed glass jars stays fresh for a long time.

Oops!

Glass cracks or shatters if it is hit or dropped. **BEWARE!** Broken glass has very sharp edges.

Making new glass

Glass is produced in a **factory**. It is not a **natural material**.

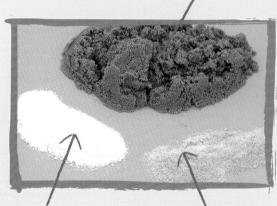

silica sand

soda ash (a chemical)

limestone (crushed, chalky rock)

The raw ingredients

Glass is made mostly of pure sand called silica. This is mixed with limestone and soda ash and heated in a **furnace** to 1,600°C (2,900°F).

The inside of a furnace

amber cullet

green cullet

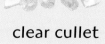

clear cullet

Soda ash lowers the melting **temperature** of the sand. Limestone makes the glass stronger. Some **cullet** (crushed, recycled glass) is also added. This is of the same type and colour as the finished glass. It helps the mixture **melt** more quickly.

Poured, pressed and pulled

Molten glass is hot, soft and flexible. It can be poured, blown, pressed, pulled or put in a **mould** to make almost any shape.

handblown jug

moulded jar

Once glass has been shaped, it is left to cool. As it cools, glass becomes hard and strong and stays in its particular shape.

LOOK AND SEE

How many different glass jars can you find? The shapes help products to stand out from one another.

Returning glass bottles

Most empty glass jars and bottles are thrown away. However, getting rid of glass is a problem.

Burn, bury or break down?

Glass cannot be burned. If it is buried at a **landfill site** it takes up a lot of space. Glass does not **rot**, so it also spoils the **environment**. Since it is easy to wash glass and use it again and again, it is a real waste to throw it away.

Back to sender

Some companies sell soft drinks to shops, cafés and bars in returnable glass bottles.

They collect the empty bottles and return them to a bottling plant to be washed, **sterilised**, refilled, labelled, capped and sold again.

Why re-use glass?

Re-using glass bottles uses less **energy** than melting old bottles to make new ones or making new bottles from scratch.

A fair exchange

In some places, you cannot buy a new bottled drink unless you bring back an empty bottle in exchange.

Elsewhere, for example in this Egyptian shop, you pay an extra amount for the bottle.

This is called a deposit. When you return the empty bottle you get the deposit back.

Re-using glass

We should save glass jars and bottles whenever we can.

Use it again

Some jars and bottles are designed to be used as something else once they are empty. See how many you can spot in supermarkets and shops.

Chocolate spread and mustard jars can become drinking glasses.

Vinegar bottles can be used as small jugs for salad dressing.

A coffee jar can become an airtight storage jar.

Ready to refill

Glass jars can be used
again and again.

Instead of buying new glass jars
of herbs and spices, you could
refill empty ones.

Wash small, empty jars and
their lids. Use them for
storing buttons, paperclips,
drawing pins or coins.

*Try decorating empty jars
with painted patterns
or glue on paper
scraps
or old
stamps.*

*Use them as containers for
pencils and paintbrushes.*

13

Decorated bottles

In Morocco, some craftsworkers turn all sorts of discarded bottles into something new.

Delightful drizzlers

The craftsmen collect small, empty juice bottles. They cover the base with beaten metal and make a new metal spout and top. The bottles become drizzlers for pouring oil on salads.

juice bottle

oil drizzler

Silvery sprinklers

Other craftsmen buy old perfume bottles. They decorate them with metal designs and add a new long, twisted metal spout. These are used as rosewater sprinklers to make rooms smell sweet.

perfume bottle ➡

sprinkler

sprinkler

Stunning spice jars

Just by adding a new metal base and lid, medicine jars are changed into spice jars.

medicine jar ➡ spice jar

Pretty pepperpots

Look how this bottle neck has been turned into a pepperpot. It has a new metal base and lid.

bottle neck ➡ pepperpot

Cut glass

In South Africa, some craftspeople make **tumblers** and vases from empty bottles.

Turning out a tumbler

1. A craftsman scratches a line in a bottle with a sharp cutter, which is set at exactly the right height for a tumbler.

2. He fills the bottle up to the scored line with hot water.

3. Then he turns the bottle under cold water and the bottle cracks in two.

4. To finish off the tumbler, the craftsman smoothes the rough, cut edge.

Two for the price of one

Bottles like those below can be turned into a fine cut glass tumbler and an unusual vase.

The bottom part of the clear bottle becomes the tumbler.

The top part is turned upside-down and glued to the upside-down base of the blue bottle.

Look! A new vase.

All change

People have thought up clever ways to re-use things made of glass.

Charming candlesticks

These candlesticks are made from upturned bottles with their bases cut off. The necks stand in a new metal base. The cut rim is trimmed with a ring of metal.

A perfect platter

A whole bottle has been slowly heated and flattened to make this glass plate.

A crazy chandelier

Old drinking glasses and cups are part of this sparkling chandelier. What other pieces of glass can you see? What kitchen utensils can you spot as well?

A green goblet

Can you work out what parts of a bottle this **goblet** is made from?

Recycling glass

If you do not want to keep old bottles and jars – **recycle** them.

Why bother to recycle?

Recycling glass reduces the amount of waste in landfill. Re-using cullet in the furnace saves taking more raw materials out of the Earth to make new glass. Cullet also melts at a lower temperature than raw ingredients, so this saves energy in heating the furnace as well.

Household collection

If the local council collects from your home, put out jars as well as bottles in the box or bag that they provide.

Bottle banks

Otherwise, put glass into bottle banks. Make sure you put each colour glass into the correct bottle bank. Clear glass is recycled into all sorts of containers. Green glass is made mainly into wine bottles.

As good as new

Most bottles and jars are made with more than a third of recycled glass. There is no difference between a recycled bottle or jar and a new one. Recycled glass is just as clean and pure as new glass.

IT'S A FACT

You cannot recycle every kind of glass. Remember: do NOT put any of these things into recycling bins:
- ✗ light bulbs
- ✗ mirrors
- ✗ glass bowls or cups
- ✗ heatproof glass dishes

YOU CAN HELP

Before you recycle jars and bottles:
- empty and rinse them
- remove any plastic or metal tops and lids
- sort the bottles by colour into clear, brown and green glass (put blue glass with green glass)
- put them into strong bags for carrying to the bottle bank

Take the bag back home with you and re-use that as well!

New glass from old

Lorries take glass from bottle banks to a **recycling plant**.

Crushed into cullet

Lorries tip their loads on to different coloured piles of glass. The glass is put on to a hopper and fed on to a conveyor belt. Here people sort the glass by hand, picking out any plastic and cork. Then the glass is crushed into cullet.

Heap of cleaned green cullet

Cullet cleaning

Magnets remove any metal caps or lids from the cullet. Vacuum cleaners suck away paper labels.

Lasers find other waste, such as pottery. Jets of air blow this away. Finally, the cullet is ready for the furnace.

Making bottles

Machines make bottles in two different moulds.

1. A **gob** of molten glass drops into the first mould. Air is blown in to create the neck and then the rough shape of a bottle, known as a **parison**.

2. The parison is transferred into the second mould. Air blown into this mould inflates the bottle into its final shape

parison

bottle

3. If glass cools fast it becomes **brittle**. To make bottles strong, they are reheated and cooled slowly in a tunnel called a lehr. This process is called annealing.

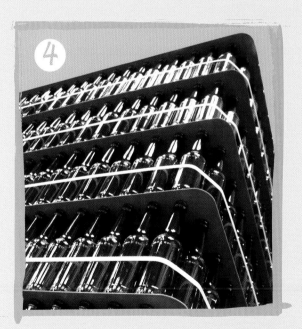

4. The bottles are sent to food or drinks factories where they are filled, labelled and capped. Then they are sold to shops.

Glass blowing

In many countries, glassblowers make all sorts of amazing glass objects.

Making glass by hand

1. The furnace is filled with recycled glass. This is far cheaper than using raw materials.

2. The glassblower picks up a gob of molten glass on the end of an iron tube. He blows down the tube and the glass forms a bubble.

3. While the glass is still hot, he quickly shapes it with tools. Then he puts it in a cooler part of the furnace to cool slowly.

Really recycled

All these objects have been hand-blown, using 100% recycled glass bottles.

This lampshade is made of coloured glass balls.

A fruit dish

A drinking glass

A vase

A bowl

Glass galore

People have discovered many ways to recycle glass.

Tumbled glass

Sometimes, bottles, TV screen glass and test tubes are crushed together. The pieces are tumbled to smooth their edges. They are used to make paths, pools and fountains that glisten and sparkle.

Beautiful beads

Some white glass cosmetic pots are melted and pressed into beads. Tiny amounts of ground metal, called oxides, are added to the molten glass. These colour the beads.

cosmetic pot

Terrific glass tiles

To make glass tiles, green, brown, blue and clear bottles are broken into cullet of different sizes – large, medium or small. The cullet is carefully arranged in square moulds. The moulds are heated slowly in a kiln. Here, the glass melts just enough for the pieces of cullet to join together into a solid tile block.

Patterned glass tiles like this one have been set at intervals into a pathway to show pedestrians the route to a river side.

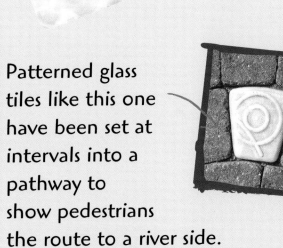

The clear glass tiles above were set into the pavement of a town shopping centre. They have lights underneath, so they glow at night.

Glossary

brittle easily broken

cullet crushed pieces of waste glass which are recycled

energy the power that drives machines

environment the world around us – the land, sea and air

factory a building where things are made in large numbers using machines

furnace a large enclosed oven lined with bricks where glass or metal is melted at a very high temperature

gob a measured lump of soft, molten glass

goblet a drinking glass with a big cup and a stem

hygienic clean, germ-free

landfill site a huge pit in the ground where crushed rubbish is buried

liquid a runny substance, such as water, that has no shape of its own

magnet a piece of iron that has the power to attract steel and other pieces of iron to it

material a substance used to make something else

melt to turn from a solid into a liquid

molten glass hot, melted, liquid glass

mould a hollowed out shape. If molten glass is poured into a mould, it takes on the shape of the mould.

natural material a material made by nature not by people

parison the name given to the first shape of a glass bottle

recycle to use an existing object or material to make something new, instead of throwing it away

recycling plant a place where waste glass is delivered and sorted for recycling

re-use to use again

rot the natural way a material slowly breaks down into lots of smaller, different substances

sterilise to make something completely free from germs

temperature a measure of how hot or cold something is

tumbler a large drinking glass with straight sides

Guess what?

- It takes a million years for glass to rot.

- Between 8 and 10 per cent of the weight of your household rubbish is glass.

- On average, every family in the UK uses around 500 glass containers (bottles or jars) per year.

- A modern glass factory can produce 2,000 bottles a minute.

- The energy saved by recycling one glass bottle will power a computer for 25 minutes.

- Only 35% of all glass in the UK is currently recycled.

Useful websites

British Glass
www.recyclingglass.co.uk
A free CD ROM and video about glass can be ordered via the website

Rockware Glass
www.glassforever.co.uk
Offers school visits, a free mobile roadshow and resource packs for KS2

Green Bottle Unit
www.freeform.org.uk
Provides design workshops to schools on tile making

www.ollierecycles.com
A fun, interactive site for children about recycling

www.recyclemore.co.uk
Help and advice on recycling at home and at school

www.thomasrecycling.com
Tips, facts and information on recycling

www.wasteonline.org.uk
Downloadable information sheets on recycling glass

www.epa.gov/kids/garbage.htm
Games and ideas about recycling in general

www.recyclezone.org.uk
Activities, games and information on recycling

Index